Jackson's Book Report

by Wyatt Taylor
illustrated by Ken Bowser

Harcourt
SCHOOL PUBLISHERS

Printed in China

ISBN 10: 0-15-351509-0
ISBN 13: 978-0-15-351509-5

Ordering Options
ISBN 10: 0-15-351213-X (Grade 3 Advanced Collection)
ISBN 13: 978-0-15-351213-1 (Grade 3 Advanced Collection)
ISBN 10: 0-15-358099-2 (package of 5)
ISBN 13: 978-0-15-358099-4 (package of 5)

5 6 7 8 9 10 985 12 11 10 09

I admit that I'm a great reader. I read anything I can and I have a good memory, too. I remember almost everything I read. I'm pretty good at school. I think that's because I read well. You'd think that means school is easy for me, but it isn't always!

One problem is that when the school year begins, I can't wait to read all the stories in my new reading book. After about a month, I've read all the stories for the whole year. That kind of takes the excitement out of things. I have been known to daydream in class. I try to pay attention, but my mind wanders. Also, because I know the stories already, I tend to put off doing assignments that go with them. Sometimes I wait too long or even forget about them.

The other problem is that I don't like to talk in class. I'm not sure why. Sometimes I'll sit at my desk and watch classmates struggle for answers. I usually know the answer, but I still don't raise my hand. If I get called on, I know everyone in the room will be looking at me. I'll get flustered and forget things and mumble. Sometimes Mr. Knoll asks me to repeat myself. That makes matters worse, so I try to lie low.

When Mr. Knoll announced an oral book report, my mind went in two ways at once. On the one hand, I would get to read a new book. We had to pick a book from outside the classroom. He didn't care what book we chose, although he did want to know what it was. You could get it from the school library or the public library or wherever you wanted. He offered help choosing a book, but I knew I didn't need it. Half the fun of reading was picking out something interesting.

On the other hand, it would mean having to go to the front of the room and speak. Mr. Knoll said you could take notes up with you, but you were not supposed to just read something you'd written. You had to speak. I don't even like talking in class, so the idea of going up and having my classmates staring at me while I talked filled me with dread.

What got me in trouble was the date. If the book report had been due in two weeks, I might have been fine. I would have had to do it right then. Mr. Knoll, though, wanted to give everyone plenty of time. He allowed a week to select a book, two weeks to read it, and a week to get the report ready. It was a whole month away, so I thought I had plenty of time.

Anyway, I already had a book, *Fire-Hunter* by Jim Kjelgaard. My dad loved it when he was young and had found it for me in the attic.

"Kjelgaard, eh?" said Mr. Knoll. "I've read some of his books. He also wrote *Big Red*. Maybe you'd like that one."

"Well, I already have *Fire-Hunter*," I said.

"All right then, Jackson, go ahead. Get a good start, though. It might be a little long."

"I can do it," I said.

"I know you can," replied Mr. Knoll.

I meant to do it, too. The book looked really interesting, with a picture of a cave dweller facing a saber-toothed tiger on the front. I read the first few pages. The characters, Hawk and Willow, were really interesting. Then, somehow, I set it aside. The weather got warmer, and I was outside a lot. I wasn't worried. I had plenty of time. Then the book got buried in the clutter in my room.

It's not that Mr. Knoll never mentioned it. He reminded us each day. I guess I just didn't want to think about standing up there in front of the class.

Before I knew it, the date of the book report was a week away. Some of the other kids had already finished. I was in a panic. I raced home and found the book. Trembling, I turned to the back and discovered there were 218 pages! They were in small print, too.

I read like crazy. It was a good book, and I stayed up as late as my parents would allow. After a few days, though, I knew I was never going to make it.

The last day came, and I was still reading at the breakfast table and on the school bus. I was reading on the way into school. When Mr. Knoll called on me to give my report, I still had eighty pages to go.

The class looked sorry for me when I dragged myself forward because they knew I had stalled as long as possible. They could see my dread. They didn't know the half of it. I probably should have just admitted the truth right there and then.

"My book is *Fire-Hunter*, by Jim Kjelgaard,"
I began slowly. Then I started to tell the story of
Hawk and Willow, and the class seemed interested.
To my surprise, I discovered I was enjoying myself.
Hawk and Willow's struggles to survive were
exciting. There was still a problem. I had no idea
how the book ended.

I really don't know what came over me. I made
up the rest of the tale on the spot. I had a great
time. I ended with a savage battle between the
saber-toothed tiger and Hawk. I even
included a final adventure for
Willow for good measure.
The class loved it, and they
applauded as I finished.

Before recess, Mr. Knoll beckoned me over. "You know, Jackson, I don't really remember the book ending that way."

I gulped.

"You told a pretty good story," he continued. "The assignment was an oral book report. You did a great job on the oral part."

"Uh, thanks," I said. I don't know what was visible on my face, but it made him smile. "When you actually finish *Fire-Hunter*, please come to me and give the book report."

"Yes, I definitely will," I said.

"And, Jackson," Mr. Knoll said, "next time . . ."

He didn't have to explain his remark. I knew exactly what he was going to say, and I knew I would never make that mistake again!

Think Critically

1. What happened because Jackson read all the stories in his reading book at the beginning of the school year?

2. Why was having extra time not helpful to Jackson?

3. Why did the class applaud when Jackson finished his report?

4. At what point should Jackson have realized that Mr. Knoll had read *Fire-Hunter*?

5. What would you have done if you had been in Jackson's situation?

 Social Studies

Public Speaking Many famous people are known for their ability to speak in public. Abraham Lincoln was one president who was an excellent public speaker. Look on the Internet or in a history book for information about Abraham Lincoln. Then list five facts that you found about him.

School-Home Connection Ask friends and family members to tell you stories of the biggest challenges they faced in school and how they met them.

Word Count: 1,061